CONTENTS

THEIR INTENSE ORIGIN STORIES

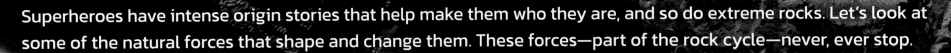

Superheroes have intense origin stories that help make them who they are, and so do extreme rocks. Let's look at some of the natural forces that shape and change them. These forces—part of the rock cycle—never, ever stop.

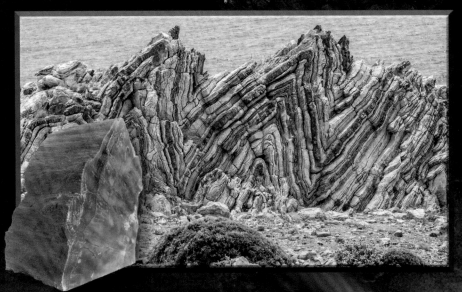

Extreme Heat!

Earth's core is an unreal 9,392 degrees F (5,200 degrees C). The mantle, made mostly of magma, surrounds that outer core. Its temperatures also range in the thousands. Intense heat causes magma to rise from the mantle to the crust, which then hardens to create igneous rocks.

Extreme Pressure!

If you have ever helped make dough, you know pressure from your hands can change its shape and help it become what it's meant to be. Pressure within Earth can change the shape or even the makeup of rocks buried within the crust.

ROCK YOUR WORLD

Intrusive igneous rocks form below the ground, while extrusive igneous rocks form above the ground, where the weather and ice keep unleashing their power on them.

Extreme Time!

In terms of geology, a hundred years is a blink of an eye. Rocks and minerals can require thousands of times more than that to form. Diamonds can be nearly as old as Earth itself!

Extreme Water and Yucky Crud!

Water wears away rock, carrying along sediment— yucky crud!—that helps form new rocks. Floods and large bodies of water can carve mountains!

THESE ROCKS SCREAM EXTREME!

There is rain, and then there are *downpours*. There are waves, and then there are *tsunamis*, waves so big they can wash away cars and buildings. There is snow, and then there are *blizzards*. In the same way, there are rocks, and then there are *extreme rocks*.

Extreme rocks have extreme characteristics and origins—some amazing, some terrifying—but all rocks come in three basic types:

1 IGNEOUS ROCK forms when magma or lava from a volcano cools.

2 SEDIMENTARY ROCK forms from sediment left behind by wind or water.

3 METAMORPHIC ROCK forms when heat or pressure changes sedimentary or igneous rock.

Rocks contain minerals, which are found in nature and are not made from living things. The minerals within rocks give them their colors and help them be their extreme best.

And here's a fun fact: We live on an extreme rock! This third rock from the sun that we call "Earth" weighs about 6 sextillion tons (5.4 sextillion tonnes)! That's a six followed by **21 zeros**. Our planet's rock layers go hundreds of miles deep.

Its surface is made up of floating plates of rock that constantly move. Sometimes they crash together and cause volcanoes or earthquakes. And sometimes those forces become the intense origin stories of extreme rocks.

Now that we've talked about what makes rocks extreme, let's meet some of the most extreme on the planet—and beyond!

EARTH

ROCK YOUR WORLD

CONGLOMERATE ROCKS are a special type of sedimentary rock. You could call them the rocky road ice cream of the rock world. They contain pieces of sedimentary, igneous, or metamorphic rock held together by sand or mud.

SEPTARIAN NODULES

Formed in the days when dinosaurs roamed Earth, these oddball rocks look like turtle shells on the outside. Inside you'll find a surprise—about seven of them, in fact.

Septarian nodules are the products of **death** and **destruction**—the shells of dead marine creatures and volcanic activity. They get their name from the Latin word for "seven," referring to the seven points going in every direction. But that's not the really surprising part.

Under normal indoor light, the cracks can appear dull in color. But look at them under ultraviolet light, and you'll see something very different.

The cracks fluoresce, or glow, under UV light. They also become phosphorescent, which means they continue to shine a strange colored light all on their own even after the light is off. What was once tan or brown becomes a spellbinding blue or green.

Septarian nodules get a double portion of glow power from two fluorescing minerals: calcite and aragonite. Calcite glows in a rainbow of colors, while aragonite glows in a ghostly, ghastly green or white.

SEPTARIAN NODULE
Under regular light.

SEPTARIAN NODULE
Under UV light.

ROCK YOUR WORLD

Septarian nodules are also called dragon eggs because of their egg shape and their cracked surfaces, which look like lizard skin.

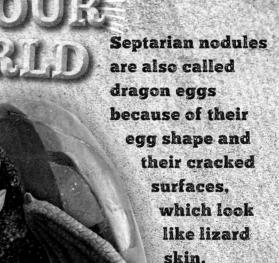

EXTREME-O-METER

EXTREME SCORE **3** GLOW POWER AND LIZARD-LIKENESS

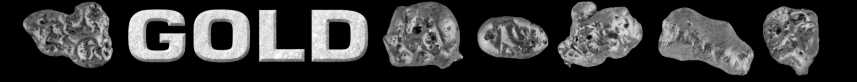

GOLD

Gold is stuff that makes bling sing! It's sparkly, shiny, and oh-so useful—not just in jewelry but also in electronics, dentistry, and even food.

It's found on all seven continents, yet all the gold in the whole world could fill only three Olympic-sized pools. Truth is, it isn't easy to find. People have died trying.

One of the things that makes gold so special is how it came to be. Scientists think gold originally came from space as stars exploded, sending clouds with gold dust toward what would become Earth.

Gold is found in veins of rocks that should come with flashing "danger" signs, like around volcanoes or places with super-hot liquid. Earthquakes create cracks in the ground that fill with water, leaving behind gold deposits.

Melting glaciers can also leave behind gold deposits. Glaciers scrape across the earth as they travel, collecting gold that was pushed to the surface by volcanoes and erosion.

ROCK YOUR WORLD

The mineral pyrite is the ultimate faker. It looks like gold, it's found near gold, but it isn't gold. One ton (0.9 tonnes) of pyrite could contain as much as $100,000 in gold. But believe it or not, extracting the gold from the pyrite may not be worth the cost.

PYRITE

GOLD

EXTREME-O-METER

EXTREME SCORE 7 DANGEROUS AND SPACEY ORIGINS

PETRIFIED WOOD

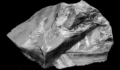

Long ago, while dinosaurs still roamed Earth, what is now an Arizona, USA, desert was once a thick forest filled with huge trees. These trees stood nearly 200 ft. (61 m) tall with trunks up to 9 ft. (2.7 m) across. They grew in a warm, wet climate like Hawaii, USA, has today. But then something happened.

Storms came. Rivers flooded. Volcanoes erupted—over and over again. Some of the trees were buried in sediment. Some were buried in volcanic ash. Even though the trees died, the sediment and ash helped to preserve some of them.

The sediment and ash contained the mineral silica. The silica combined with other minerals from groundwater and slowly replaced the cells

in the wood to make a beautiful new thing. The trees were no longer wood. They were transformed into **petrified** wood, a colorful quartz that preserved the look of the wood, including its growth rings.

← GROWTH RINGS

Arizona's Petrified Forest National Park isn't the only place where petrified wood is found. It's also found in other parts of the western United States, as well as in Tennessee, USA, and Australia. At most places visitors can only look and not touch.

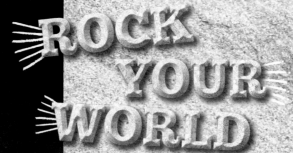

ROCK YOUR WORLD

Rocks can preserve the history of animals as well as plants. The same process that transformed ancient trees into quartz also can turn the bones or shells of animals into stone. Minerals from the groundwater help form cement that changes the bone into rock over time.

EXTREME-O-METER

EXTREME SCORE **4**   *ROCKING WHAT WAS ONCE LIFE*

CANYONS, CAVERNS, AND CAVES

If you changed the game "rock, paper, scissors" into "rock, paper, water," of course the water would beat the paper. But it would also beat the rock. That's what it does in nature—over and over and over—to create amazing and beautiful natural wonders.

Canyons, caverns, and caves are a perfect example. Canyons like the Grand Canyon result from bodies of water eroding the rock over many centuries. They can form around rivers or seas, or even under the sea.

GRAND-CANYON, ARIZONA, USA

THIEN CUNG CAVE, VIETNAM

Caves and their bigger siblings, caverns, often result when carbon dioxide—the gas that makes your soda bubbly, later causing you to burp—mixes with water and slowly erodes sedimentary rock. But some form as lava tubes, tunnels formed by sizzling hot molten lava! Still others result from other extreme forces like extreme wind or extreme ice.

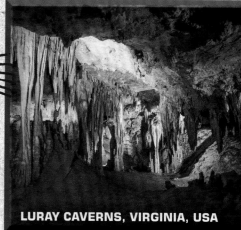
LURAY CAVERNS, VIRGINIA, USA

Inside caves and caverns, long gnarled fingers of rock known as stalactites and stalagmites grow from the ceiling and the cave floor as mineral-rich water drips from above. Stalactites should come with a "danger" sign: Like icicles in the winter, they can randomly fall and cause serious harm!

CAVE IN OKINAWA, JAPAN

These strange natural marvels turn out to be pretty useful. Canyons provide habitats for many animal species, some endangered. They also help preserve the fossil record. And canyons, caverns, and caves all act as nature's storm drains.

UNDERWATER CANYON, HUAHINE ISLAND, FRENCH POLYNESIA

DIAMONDS

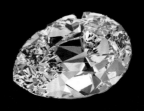

Terrifying but beautiful things happen deep within Earth's mantle, home of mind-blowing pressure and heat. There, diamonds form at temperatures ranging from 2,200 to 2,700 degrees F (1,204 to 1,482 degrees C) and at pressures that would squish a tall tower to fit onto a postage stamp.

Made of pure carbon, diamonds are the result of all that heat and pressure. It's the world's hardest mineral and is used to cut through absolutely *anything*. Most diamonds, in fact, are used in all kinds of incredible ways—in treating cancer, in making audio equipment, and as a part in dental drills. But some are just enjoyed for their beauty.

Clear diamonds may be the most popular, but diamonds come in a rainbow of colors. Believe it or not, that rainbow comes from impurities within

EARTH'S MANTLE

303 CARAT DIAMOND!

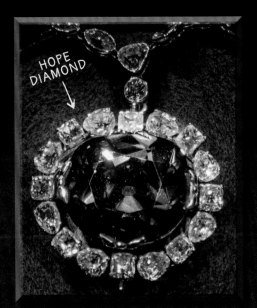
HOPE DIAMOND

diamonds. One of the world's most famous colored stones is the Hope Diamond, a massive blue rock that is believed to curse everyone who touches it.

Not everyone can have a pricey mineral like the Hope Diamond—and maybe that's a good thing, with the curse and all—but anyone can hunt for diamonds. At Crater of Diamonds State Park in Arkansas, USA, visitors pay a park entry fee to scour a volcanic crater for gemstones. And the park fee may be worth it, because any diamond they find, they get to keep!

ROCK YOUR WORLD

Diamonds may be the hardest mineral on Earth, but they have competition from an *alien*. That alien is lonsdaleite, a mineral found in meteorites. Think of it as a space diamond but harder. Sorry, diamonds!

EXTREME-O-METER

TOUGH, USEFUL, SPARKLE, AND BEAUTY

MOON AND MARS ROCKS

Rocks are not only found here on Earth. They also make up other planets, as well as our moon.

Astronauts from NASA's Apollo moon missions brought back more than 800 lbs. (363 kg) of lunar rock for scientists to study. Scientists believe the moon began as a ball of *searing-hot* molten rock.

As a result, most of the moon's surface is made of igneous rock, formed as lava cooled.

Basalt, also found on Earth, is one of the most common rocks found there. And then there's breccia, another rock found here, which resulted as meteorites smashed onto the moon's surface.

LUNAR BRECCIA

EARTH BRECCIA

EARTH BASALT

LUNAR BASALT

The meteorites also created pools of glass as they melted nearby rocks at impact.

Scientists have also been able to study rocks on Mars using NASA's uncrewed rovers. And Martian rocks tell a very interesting story. Some appear sedimentary, and others contain pebbles like conglomerate rocks. Both types point to water on Mars' surface. And where there's water, scientists believe there could be life. Could Martians exist?!

Martian rock

ROCK YOUR WORLD

We already know some rocks can be found on both Earth and the moon. Add anorthosite, one of the oldest types of rock found on the moon, to that list. But the anorthosite samples found on Earth are so much like lunar rocks that they give scientists plenty of clues about the moon's makeup and history without having to make a trip there.

EARTH ANORTHOSITE

MOON ANORTHOSITE

EXTREME-O-METER

EXTREME SCORE 8 ALIEN ORIGINS

METEORITES

Some extreme rocks are dangerous, and sometimes they fall from the sky. Meteorites are space rocks that crash into Earth, many times as blazing balls of fire. Most burn up before they hit the ground—most, but not all.

The Murchison Meteorite, which fell in Australia, is the most studied—and the most weird. Think *dirty*, *sweaty sneakers* found in a cattle yard, and you get an idea of the smell of this funky find. Found in a cow pasture, the meteorite reeks because it contains organic matter including the building blocks of DNA. Scientists think it may help them understand the origins of life.

Meteorites give scientists all kinds of clues about the universe. Some meteorites are made of rock and contain some of the oldest stuff found in our solar system.

MURCHISON METEORITE

Some are super-heavy and magnetic because they're made of metal. All contain clues about how planets and stars came to be.

Meteorite impacts are actually pretty common. Every year, somewhere between 500 and 2,000 meteorites hit Earth. Most fall into the ocean or in remote areas. (Phew!) But every 2,000 years or so, a meteorite **as big as a car** will make its way through the atmosphere and destroy everything in its path—and **beyond**—as it crashes to the ground.

Scientists believe a meteor as big as 8 mi. (13 km) across is to blame for wiping out the dinosaurs, along with most other life, after its impact in Mexico's Yucatan Peninsula.

ROCK YOUR WORLD

Even though meteorites hit Earth all the time, they're not all that easy to find. Scientists even have a word for rocks people mistake for meteorites: *meteor-wrongs*. Real meteorites are heavy for their size, are often magnetic, have weird shapes, and are covered in a thin crust. Meteor-wrongs can contain bubbles, light-colored crystals, or streaks.

METEORITE

METEOR-WRONG

EXTREME-O-METER

EXTREME SCORE **10**

POTENTIAL EXTINCTION EVENTS FROM OUTER SPACE

MOLDAVITE, LIBYAN DESERT GLASS, AND PALLASITE

Yes, meteorite impacts can destroy everything and everyone around them. But beautiful things can happen too, like moldavite and Libyan desert glass. Both resulted when meteorites hit Earth and melted the surrounding rock.

Libyan desert glass is found in Egypt near the border with Libya. The yellow stone is so beautiful that it was used on King Tut's breastplate, which was buried in his tomb. Found among sand dunes, the glass is made of silica, a mineral that only forms under extreme heat.

Moldavite, which varies in color from yellow to greenish brown, formed when a meteorite slammed into Eastern Europe, sending pieces of rock flying into the air throughout the region. The rock cooled into glass, something pretty enough to be used in jewelry.

LIBYAN DESERT GLASS

MOLDAVITE

PALLASITE

Pallasite, however, has an out-of-this-world origin story because it **is** from out of this world. Scientists believe the alien-green rock formed long, long ago—maybe in a galaxy far, far away—when an asteroid crashed into a planet. Then the newly formed rock made its way to Earth, where it is a favorite among scientists and collectors.

ROCK YOUR WORLD

Using their mad STEM skills, scientists have created a copy of a mineral found only in meteorites called tetrataenite.

TETRATAENITE

The space-inspired mineral can be used in magnets found within high-tech machines. What makes this such a big deal is it could help protect our planet by reducing the need for mining. Green for the win!

IN FEBRUARY 2023, Residents in Texas, USA, heard a loud BOOM! as a nearly 1,000 lb. (453.6-kg) meteorite crashed to the ground. No damage or injuries were reported. Phew!

EXTREME-O-METER

EXTREME SCORE 9.5 BEAUTY THAT RESULTS FROM SUPER-HOT DESTRUCTION

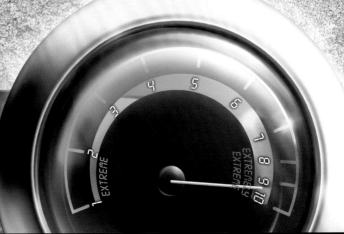

STRIKING IT RICH— OR NOT

In 2015, an Australian man used his metal detector to search for gold. He found a large, heavy brown rock that just had to have gold inside—or so he thought. He tried opening it with a sledgehammer. He tried drilling into it. He dropped it into acid. But the giant rock wasn't ready to reveal its secrets.

Finally he got the help of experts, who sawed it open with a diamond. The giant rock turned out to be an ancient meteorite even more valuable than gold because of its rarity and its value to science. The meteorite's tightly held secrets may help experts learn how the universe came to be.

MELBORNE MUSEUM, AUSTRALIA

Sometimes people are able to cash in on their otherworldly finds. A bean-sized piece of meteorite found in Winchcombe, England, sold in 2022 for $12,600, far more than the value of the same amount of gold.

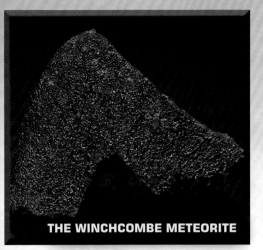

THE WINCHCOMBE METEORITE

Sometimes people don't strike it rich as is the case with the owners of Roky the German shepherd. In good news, Roky was perfectly okay after his doghouse in Costa Rica was hit by a tiny meteorite in 2019. In bad news, his family didn't get anywhere near what they hoped the meteorite was worth.

ROCK YOUR WORLD

Some meteorites may be worth more than their weight in gold, but nothing compares with the asteroid 16 Psyche. Scientists believe the giant space rock may be worth as much as $10,000 quadrillion–that's one followed by 19 zeros!–because of the gold and other metals within it. NASA plans to send an uncrewed spacecraft to study the asteroid.

ASTEROID PSYCHE

GLACIER ICE

So what's the coolest rock of all? It HAS to be glacier ice! At its most basic definition, a metamorphic rock forms when any solid material changes into another solid form as the result of forces in nature. That means when snowflakes turn into ice crystals that come together as a glacier, that glacier—a river of ice that flows downhill—is actually a rock!

Glacier ice requires extreme time, as in hundreds or thousands of years, to form. It all begins with snowflakes. Snow collects on the ground, trapping air between the flakes to create the fluffy stuff we all love so much.

As more snow falls—and little to none of it melts—the snow gets packed down, squeezing

ROCK YOUR WORLD

Sheets of natural ice may be metamorphic rock, but the ice cubes that form in your freezer are not. Metamorphic rocks can only be created in nature without any help from humans.

Unlike other metamorphic rocks, though, glacier ice is always on the move. Gravity pulls it downhill. It can move fast down steep slopes or more slowly down gentler ones. The bigger the glacier, the faster it moves! The world's fastest glacier covers most of Greenland. It travels an average of 130 ft. (39.6 m) a day!

out the air between the flakes and forming a solid sheet of ice. Just like with other metamorphic rocks, the minerals within the glacier ice rearrange themselves into a new thing.

EXTREME-O-METER

EXTREME SCORE 8.5 COOL FACTOR

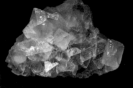

FLUORITE

GREEN AND PURPLE FLUORITE

Imagine having an ability so amazing that it's named after you. Meet fluorite, from which we get the term "fluorescent." Fluorite fluoresces, or glows, a spooky blue under ultraviolet light. In regular light, it often appears yellow, pink, green, orange, blue, or purple, sometimes with rainbow stripes of color.

On its own, fluorite is clear and colorless like glass. But impurities often mix with it as it forms in extreme heat—near hot springs or in cracks in rock that bubble up with hot water pushed up from deep within Earth. The impurities make fluorite pretty enough to use in jewelry. But because it breaks easily, it must be worn with care.

FLUORITE UNDER ULTRA-VIOLET LIGHT

PINK FLUORITE

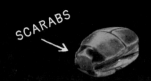

SCARABS

Ancient Egyptians carved fluorite into statues and scarabs. In China, people have also used it in carvings—as well as in medicine. Ancient Chinese would mix powdered fluorite with water to treat kidney disease. It turns out the Chinese were a little ahead of their time in using fluorite as medicine.

Fluorite is still used in medicine today. In fact, it's used in **many** surprising ways: in plastics, metals,

ROCK YOUR WORLD

Fluorite is the source of fluoride, used in toothpaste and mouthwash to prevent cavities and make teeth stronger. Some communities add fluoride to tap water to improve people's dental health.

pottery, toothpaste, weed killer, dyes, glass, lenses for glasses, cleaning products, rocket fuel, products for preventing stains, items that keep things cold, and in concrete. It would be hard to imagine our world without it!

EXTREME-O-METER

EXTREME SCORE 8 GLOW POWER, SMILE POWER, AND USEFUL

 MAGNETITE

Magnetite looks nothing like fluorite, but the two have something in common. Like fluorite, magnetite has a special ability named for it—in this case, magnetism. Magnets are useful for more than picking up paper clips or nails. They're used in gadgets like cellphones, computers, and even cars.

NAILS ON MAGNETITE

MAGNET ON MAGNETITE

Magnetite, which is found in many types of rocks, is nature's own backup drive. Within it, scientists can find information about Earth's magnetic field at the time its crystals were formed.

Like other extreme rocks, magnetite has a pretty nifty origin story. Legend has it that it gets its name from an ancient Greek shepherd boy named Magnes. He noticed the iron in his staff and the nails in his shoes bending toward the rock he stood on while he tended his sheep.

Magnes wasn't the only person in the ancient world to notice magnetite's extreme skills. The ancient Chinese would hang a type of magnetite from a string to use as a compass.

MINING MAGNETITE

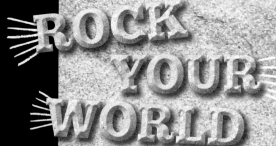

If we picture a beach, we imagine tan sand against blue-green water. But sand isn't always tan. Sometimes it's black, like at the Great Sand Dunes in Colorado, USA, or beaches in Hawaii, USA and New Zealand. The black color comes from magnetite in the sand. So instead of taking a shovel and pail for playing in the sand, take a magnet!

Finding magnetite may be easier than you think because it isn't just found in the earth. It's found in living things like bacteria, bird beaks, fish noses, and **human brains**.

It's possible that magnetite may act as an internal compass that helps animals migrate long distances to the same locations time and time again. This ability is known as magnetoreception—a second word named after magnetite!

HANA, HAWAII, USA

EXTREME-O-METER

EXTREME SCORE 8.5 MAGNETIC PERSONALITY

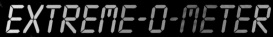

29

AUTUNITE

Some things just scream "**touch me**," like puppies and kittens and things with interesting textures. The mineral autunite appears to be covered in moss, making some people want to touch it. But don't—**just don't**.

DON'T TOUCH!!!

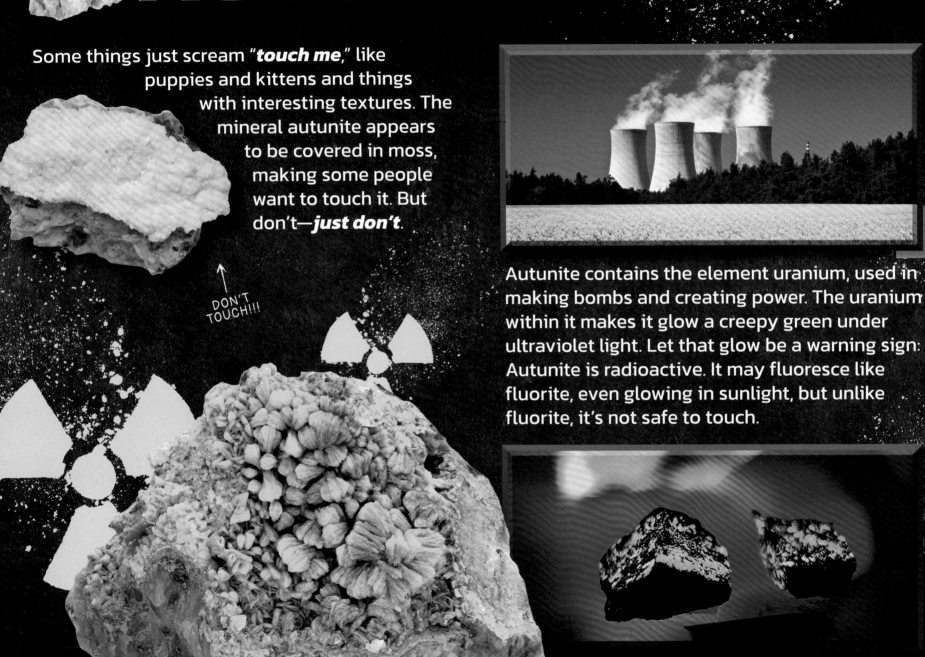

Autunite contains the element uranium, used in making bombs and creating power. The uranium within it makes it glow a creepy green under ultraviolet light. Let that glow be a warning sign: Autunite is radioactive. It may fluoresce like fluorite, even glowing in sunlight, but unlike fluorite, it's not safe to touch.

Because it's so interesting and glows in such a wild way, autunite is a favorite among rock and mineral collectors. But collectors must be very careful when storing it. Autunite can't be stored in a house—too dangerous. It can't be stored in a sealed container. That causes radiation to build up. And it needs to be kept in a moist atmosphere to preserve it.

Not surprisingly, autunite is used to create nuclear power and in electrical devices. It was once used to create reddish-yellow glazes used on ceramic items. Such items are now mostly off-limits because, though pretty, they may also be *pretty deadly*.

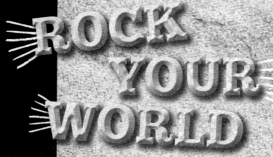

ROCK YOUR WORLD

The element lead can also cause serious illness, but the lead-based mineral galena managed to change the world for the better. Galena can conduct electricity, as well as extract music and voices from radio waves. In the early 1900s, it became the key to crystal radios, which brought news and entertainment to the entire world.

EXTREME-O-METER

EXTREME SCORE 10   INTERNAL DEATH RAYS

VOLCANIC GLASS

Sometimes two kids from the same parents will look nothing alike. That's true of obsidian and pumice, two types of volcanic glass that couldn't look more different!

But are obsidian and pumice rocks, or are they glass? They're both! But only one of them **looks** like glass.

Obsidian results when lava cools really fast. It's usually black, though impurities can sometimes turn it reddish brown. But even with its dark color, it's so shiny that Aztecs and ancient Greeks used it as a mirror! It's also sharp enough to be used in weapons and tools.

Pumice, however, isn't the tiniest bit shiny.

OBSIDIAN GLASS DAGGER

OBSIDIAN

PUMICE

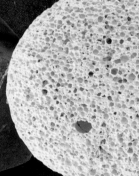

It's dull and full of tiny holes, with its surface kind of looking like bubbles you blow into your milk. Like milk, it is often a creamy white.

It forms when magma spews from Earth in a bubbly froth like a soft drink. Then it cools fast, before the gas bubbles can pop. The holes left behind give pumice an extreme skill: It can float in water! Entire islands made of pumice formed by underwater volcanoes have floated across oceans!

FLOATING PUMICE

BLUE OBSIDIAN

ROCK YOUR WORLD

Because the idea of volcanoes isn't scary enough, volcanoes have stepped up the terror factor a notch.

They can send volcanic *bombs*—red-hot molten rocks—flying high up into the air and thousands of feet or meters away! In 2018, a Hawaiian man was injured when one flew 100 yds. (91 m), hitting his leg.

EXTREME-O-METER

EXTREME SCORE 5 RESULTING FROM SPEWING MAGMA

SERPENTINE

It's no accident that "serpent" is part of serpentine's name. This mineral is slippery like snakeskin, it's green like some snakes, and its surface has a snakeskin-like pattern to it. But the name doesn't describe just one mineral. It describes a whole group of them that have those traits in common.

Snakes can sometimes be found underground, but serpentine is found **way** underground. It is the product of extreme pressure and extra heat. It begins as igneous rock pushed up from Earth's mantle on the ocean floor. Hot water from underwater volcanoes combines with shifting plates within the Earth to result in serpentine.

SERPENTINE CLOSE-UP

SNAKESKIN

Some scientists believe serpentine plays a role in creating chaos within Earth. As serpentine breaks down, it makes the area unstable because rock has room to shift. That shifting—you guessed it!—can cause earthquakes, all thanks to serpentine.

When Earth's plates crash and bang together, they can fold, creating mountains where serpentine is often found. Sometimes, as the earth continues to shift, the mineral works its way to the surface and breaks down into soil. Serpentine soil becomes home to some wildflowers, along with—gulp!—plants that eat insects and sometimes small animals.

CARNIVOROUS CALIFORNIA PITCHER PLANT

ROCK YOUR WORLD

Serpentine isn't just found around mountains or on ocean floors. It was once found in houses, schools, and other buildings. That's because it's often a source of the mineral asbestos, which can keep buildings warm in the winter and cool in the summer. Once scientists discovered that asbestos can be dangerous to humans, though, it was no longer used.

EXTREME-O-METER

EXTREME SCORE **6**

SNAKESKIN-LIKE EARTH-SHAKER

QUARTZ

The mineral quartz is almost everywhere. It's under your feet as you walk along the beach. It's found in many gemstones. It's used in watches and in electronics. And it has some serious superpowers. To explain, let's look at ketchup.

When you squeeze a ketchup bottle, ketchup comes out. We don't expect something to come out of a quartz crystal when we squeeze it, yet it does. It releases an electrical charge. That charge builds up with more pressure. This is called the piezoelectric effect. This trait makes quartz a useful part of our TVs, cellphones, and favorite electronic game consoles.

But that's not quartz's only superpower. It also protects us, as in all of us, from otherwise certain death and doom. It helps power Earth's magnetic field, which keeps us from getting fried by the sun's cosmic rays.

ROSE QUARTZ

AMETRINE

CARNELIAN

AMETHYST

CHALCEDONY

TIGER'S EYE

CITRINE

Here's how it works. A solar wind carries charged particles from the sun to Earth. If those particles reached our atmosphere, they would eat away at our ozone layer, which protects us from the sun's dangerous radiation. But our magnetic field acts like a shield against most of those particles.

Quartz may be a pretty big deal, but it can also be just plain *pretty*. It's the key mineral in many gemstones—amethyst, ametrine, citrine, chalcedony, tiger's eye, and rose quartz, to name a few. All in all, it makes the world a better, safer, and prettier place.

ROCK YOUR WORLD

Try clapping five times in just one second. Impossible, right? Now try to get your head around this. The piezoelectric effect within quartz crystals causes them to vibrate at 32,768 times per second—*per second*—allowing watches to keep perfect time.

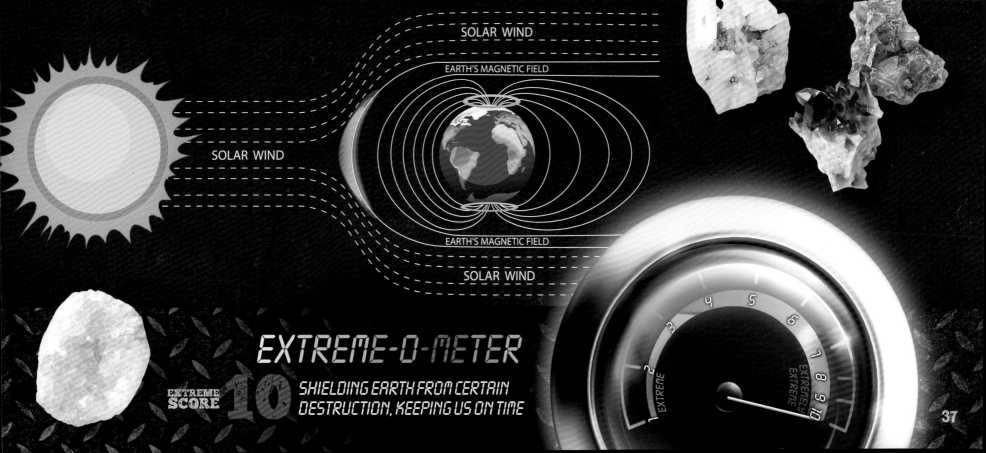

SOLAR WIND

EARTH'S MAGNETIC FIELD

SOLAR WIND

EARTH'S MAGNETIC FIELD

SOLAR WIND

EXTREME-O-METER

EXTREME SCORE 10

SHIELDING EARTH FROM CERTAIN DESTRUCTION, KEEPING US ON TIME

GEODES

Have you ever opened a plain-looking box or paper bag and found something wonderful inside? Geodes are like the plain boxes of the rock world. On the outside, they look pretty boring. That's because they hide their beauty inside.

Geodes form in igneous rock, where crystals grow from minerals within the rock. They fill holes, or cavities, left by gas bubbles. They can also form in sedimentary rock, where minerals fill cavities with the help of extreme time, pressure, space, and heat.

INSIDE AN AGATE GEODE

QUARTZ

AGATE

AGATE

AMETHYST

AMETHYST

PINK AMETHYST

CITRINE

Calcite crystals and quartz often line the insides of geodes. So do amethysts, beautiful purple gemstones. Some geodes contain even more pricey surprises like the gem opal, with its flashes of color, or pink rhodochrosite.

In 1897, miners accidentally discovered the world's largest geode, Crystal Cave in Put-in-Bay, Ohio, USA. Unlike most geodes, which are small enough to hold in your hand, this one is large enough to hold a crowd within its crystal-lined walls!

THUNDER EGGS are first cousins to geodes. The only difference is thunder eggs aren't hollow like geodes. Their insides are solid crystal.

ROCK YOUR WORLD

The Uruguay Amethyst ranks as the world's largest amethyst-filled geode. At 11 ft. (3.4 m) tall, it weighs as much as a large SUV! A museum bought it in 2007 for $75,000 and is reported to have turned down offers to buy it for several times that much!

EXTREME-O-METER

EXTREME SCORE **4** A SPARKLING SURPRISE INSIDE

CORUNDUM

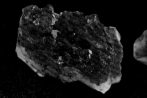

When most people think of corundum, they think of beautiful rubies and sapphires: precious and costly gems. But corundum is as tough as it is beautiful.

Second only to diamonds in hardness, corundum is used to cut through almost anything, including other gems. It's also used in the glass of telescopes, in sandpaper, and in nail files—and let's not forget space.

One of corundum's brightest moments was the invention of the ruby-powered laser in 1969.

RUBY-POWERED LASER

Scientists used the laser as a cosmic measuring tape to figure out the distance between the moon and Earth. They did this by measuring the amount of time it took for a laser pulse to travel to the moon and back again. That gave scientists all kinds of ideas about how to use ruby lasers, including in surgeries.

It turns out sapphires and rubies also make really tough glass that stands up well to heat. Sapphire glass has been used in the windows of spacecraft, which have to survive temperatures of 2,691 degrees F (1,477 degrees C) as they reenter Earth's atmosphere!

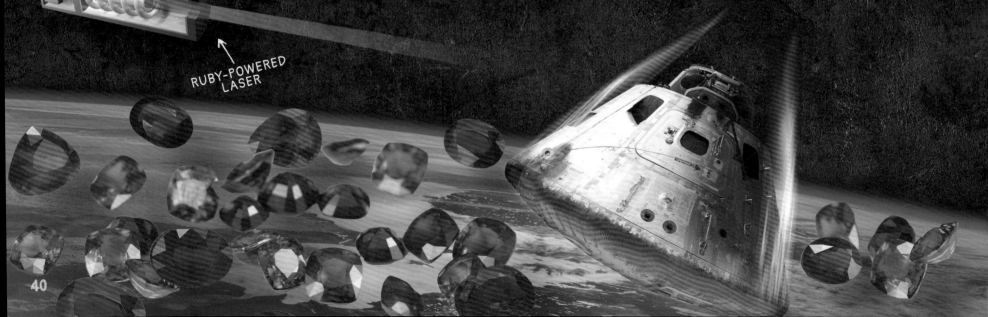

The problem is, because they're gems, sapphires and rubies cost a lot. But scientists found a way around that by copying them in a lab.

Red corundum is called a ruby, while corundum in any other color is called a sapphire. Like fluorite, rubies and some sapphires fluoresce under ultraviolet light or in strong sunlight. It turns out corundum has more than one extreme ability!

Lab-created sapphires are so tough that they're being used as face shields and armor in battle. The glass *shatters* bullets and helps soldiers see better when they use infrared gadgets that help them spot hidden dangers.

EXTREME-O-METER

EXTREME SCORE 9.5 TOUGH ENOUGH FOR SPACE AND THE BATTLEFIELD

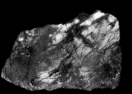

LABRADORITE

Labradorite may not look like much at first glance. But look again. Under light, its colors can appear to change depending on the angle from which it's viewed. Labradorite's special form of iridescence is called labradorescence.

The color play, also known as the schiller effect, happens as light enters the stone and reflects off its layers. The result is a brilliant display of blue, green, yellow, orange, and red—like a rainbow within a rock! Spectrolite, a type of labradorite found only in Finland, puts on the biggest color show of all. Show-off!

SPECTROLITE

RARE COLORS

Not every labradorite sample displays the schiller effect, but it still manages to be the prettiest rock in the room. A form of labradorite known as sunstone, found in Oregon, USA, is one example. The orange mineral can't lay claim to the schiller effect, but it has a trick all its own: It shimmers like glitter or stars.

ROCK YOUR WORLD

Labradorite is named for Labrador, Canada, where it is often found. Its beautiful play of color led ancient Inuits to say that the northern lights, which look a lot like labradorite's schiller effect, were trapped within the stone. Legend has it that someone hit a piece of labradorite with a spear and freed some of the northern lights. Strangely enough, labradorite can sometimes be found in the sky. That is, it's also found in meteorites.

EXTREME-O-METER

EXTREME SCORE 6 RAINBOWS, STARS, AND NORTHERN LIGHTS ALL IN ONE ROCK

WILDLY WEIRD WONDERS

Geologists study rocks so they can understand them. But some rocks just don't want to be understood.

The Eye of the Sahara

In the Sahara, a desert in Africa, there is a strange series of nesting circles 28 mi. (45 km) wide called the Eye of the Sahara whose beginnings scientists can't yet explain. Could a volcano have caused the circles to form? No clues point to one. Could an asteroid have caused the rings? The site would contain more melted rock if it were an impact crater. So what **did** cause the rings? We may never know.

Mima Mounds

Sometimes when we see a clump of trees, we know someone planted them because they're so perfectly placed. Mima mounds, found in Washington, USA, are like that. The problem is, people didn't make them. Though they look like human burial mounds, they're filled with rocks. Water and wind didn't cause them, scientists say, but maybe gophers created them. If only someone could see one there in action!

QUEBEC

Hudson Bay

Belcher Islands

ONTARIO

Nastapoka Arc

Nature is really good at creating interesting shapes but not so good at creating perfect geometric ones. That's what trips up scientists who study the Nastapoka Arc in Hudson Bay, Canada. It's nearly a perfect circle. So how did it get there? Some think it's an ancient impact crater. Or maybe the continent pulled apart long ago. Their best guess is it resulted when continents crashed together.

Scientists were stumped when rocks and boulders made mostly of the mineral dolomite seemed to propel themselves across Racetrack Playa in Death Valley National Park. Finally, experts used cameras and other tools to solve the mystery. The playa—covered in 3 in. (7 cm) of water after a winter rain had frozen overnight. As the sun rose, the cracking ice and wind sent the rocks sailing. Mystery solved!

Wind Cave

Most caves look like something from another world. But boxwork, a type of cave feature, takes strange to a whole new level. Boxwork is on full display in the Wind Cave in South Dakota, USA, where tangled webs of the mineral calcite cover layers of dolomite. Scientists believe erosion and weathering might have helped create the woven veins of rock—maybe.

THE EXTREME TEAM ROUNDUP

We've learned about mind-blowing extreme rocks—all amazing, some terrifying. Now it's time to unveil our MOST EXTREME ROCKS!

AUTUNITE

TIED FOR NO. 1 MOST EXTREME:
Autunite, Meteorites, and Quartz

It's a three-way tie for first! Autunite ranks for its internal death rays. Meteorites can cause mass-extinction events but also hold the secrets of the universe within them. And then there's quartz, which shields the world from certain destruction while keeping us on time and giving us the gadgets we so love.

QUARTZ

NO. 2 MOST EXTREME: Corundum

Corundum is beautiful enough to be used in pricey jewelry but boss enough to be used in space and in military shields.

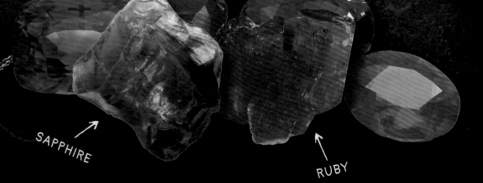

SAPPHIRE

RUBY

PALLASITE

MOLDAVITE

LIBYAN DESERT GLASS

TIED FOR NO. 3: Moldavite, Libyan Desert Glass, and Pallasite

It's hard not to love a beautiful rock formed when a meteorite melts the earth. And it's equally hard not to love one that came from space.

NO. 4: Diamonds

Extreme pressure, extreme heat, and extreme amounts of time combine to make diamonds the hardest material on Earth. And their sparkle can't be beat.

DIAMOND

TIED FOR NO. 5: Glacier Ice, Fluorite, and Alien Rocks

A metamorphic rock that forms from snowflakes and collects gold as it travels downhill? It doesn't get much cooler than glacier ice!

FLUORITE

Known for its trademark glow, fluorite makes the world a better place and makes the world smile.

The moon might have begun as a ball of searing-hot molten rock. Mars might have once had water—and *life*. These are some of the out-of-this-world things these rocks teach us.

LUNAR ROCK

MARS ROCK

Written by C. J. McDonald
Designed by Kay Petronio

© 2024 Scholastic Inc.

an imprint of

SCHOLASTIC
scholastic.com

10 9 8 7 6 5 4 3 2 1

ISBN: 978-1-546-41201-4

Printed in Guangzhou, China

OPAL THUNDER EGG